Rev Frank Armstead

1.00

A FORTRESS BOOK

THE LORD'S SUPPER

THE LORD'S SUPPER

PAST AND PRESENT PRACTICES

by

Theodore G. Tappert

A FORTRESS BOOK

FORTRESS PRESS   •   PHILADELPHIA

Printed in U.S.A.   UB2004

FOREWORD

The need for putting what we, as Christians, believe into words everybody can readily understand poses a constant challenge. In response to that challenge the New Testament itself was written in a language commonly spoken and understood. Through the ages handbooks, catechisms, and tracts have been written and, since the invention of printing, published to meet the need for clarifying in every age what it means to be a Christian.

Whether it is more difficult to be a Christian in one age than another is hard to say. But being a Christian in the second half of the twentieth century is becoming more and more complicated. This heightens the challenge of spelling out for our day in an uncomplicated way what it means to be a Christian. To put the thought patterns of theology into terms that are readily understood is not easy. Yet saying what we believe in such a way that others, without too much difficulty, will understand what we are talking about is the test of our own grasp of what we believe and hold to be true.

In tackling this task the authors of Fortress Books do not try to make a difficult faith seem easy but to make it easier for the reader to see how demanding Christian discipleship really is and how important it is for him to give meaning to what he believes in what he does.

And so the authors want to give the reader clues to guide him in making his decisions from day to day. It is the hope of the publishers that these small books, dealing with central themes of Christian faith and life, may succeed in their purpose.

Helmut T. Lehmann
Editor

CONTENTS

IDENTITY AND CHANGE

We are separated from the Last Supper which our Lord ate with his disciples in Jerusalem by a long span of time. During the more than nineteen hundred years which have passed since then, Christian people have assembled again and again in all parts of the world to eat and drink not only in commemoration of that Last Supper but especially in remembrance of him who gave it its peculiar significance. Outwardly the observance of the Lord's Supper, as we often call it, underwent a great many changes in the course of the centuries.

Such variations are not only a matter of the past. We can still observe some today. Sometimes we see the Lord's Supper in the form of an elaborate cultic act of pompous solemnity performed in a magnificent building by men arrayed in colorful vestments. Sometimes we see it in the form of a plain and unpretentious refreshment observed in utter silence by little groups of people employing ordinary vessels in unadorned buildings. A casual observer might have great difficulty in recognizing any identity in these two acts. Moreover, neither of them may seem at first sight to have very much in common with the Last Supper or with the practice of the earliest Christians.

In some respects, at least, this should not be surprising. With the passing of time and the extension of the church to the four corners of the earth, the way in which the Lord's Supper was observed was inevitably adapted to a variety of peoples and cultures. For example, in the ancient church it did not appear to be strange or offensive for people on the shores of the Mediterranean Sea to exchange a "kiss of peace" in token of Christian brotherhood when they were about to participate in the Lord's Supper. Conventions have changed long before our own day in this respect, and among fellow Christians in North America a handclasp would perhaps be a less ambiguous and therefore a more appropriate equivalent of the ancient kiss.

Not only have changes in taste and shifting modes of expression altered patterns of worship, but other factors have also played a part. Ways of observing the Lord's Supper which seemed eminently appropriate in the small assemblies of early Christians were not always suited to the larger congregations which soon emerged. Where Christians represented a minority of the population they were not always able to do what other Christians did who enjoyed the power and freedom of a majority. Various conceptions of order, leadership, and uniformity likewise had significant influence.

In any case, practices have been subject to an unending process of change. Whenever a particular usage no longer seemed to serve a real function, it was sometimes quietly dropped. It sometimes happened, however, that the usage was conservatively retained for a long time, often in an increasingly cryptic or veiled form. For example, the early exchange of kisses was in time altered to the kissing of a board (an "osculatory" or "pax-board") which was passed about among the people, and still later only the priest kissed an object, or else the entire act was finally reduced to the salutation, "The peace of the Lord be with you alway." It also happened at times that customs which had a very ordinary and practical origin were, when retained, later given allegorical meanings which had nothing whatever to do with their original function.

The gradual accumulation not only of obsolete forms but also of newly created ones threatened again and again to obscure what lies at the core of the Lord's Supper. Whenever this danger was felt to exist, protests were evoked and reforms were proposed. So the Reformers of the sixteenth century found it necessary to point out that all human traditions are bound to certain times, places, and circumstances. What may have been meaningful in one age may not be in another. It is the function of all such practices, Luther wrote, "to serve the ends of faith and love. . . . If they no longer serve such a purpose, they are already dead and gone, and they are of no value, just as . . . new shoes become old and uncomfortable and are no longer worn, but are discarded and new ones are bought."

Within the framework of changing external practices, however, Christians have been quite uniformly concerned down through the ages to observe the Supper which their Lord had instituted. In one way or another they kept before them the words of the New Testament in which this institution had been preserved. Such accounts, with a few variations in detail, have come down to us in I Cor. 11:23-25, Mark 14:22-24, Matt. 26:26-28, and Luke 22:19-20. Sometimes a conflation of these passages was used:

Our Lord Jesus Christ, on the night when he was
betrayed, took bread, and when he had given
thanks, he broke it, and gave it to the disciples
and said, "Take, eat; this is my body which is
given for you. Do this in remembrance of me." In
the same way also he took the cup, and when he
had given thanks he gave it to them, saying, "Drink
of it, all of you. This cup is the new covenant in
my blood, which is poured out for you and for
many for the forgiveness of sins. Do this, as often
as you drink it, in remembrance of me."

From early times the observance was given a variety
of names. In the New Testament itself various appella-
tions are suggested. For example, in Acts 2:42 there
is reference to "the breaking of bread," in I Cor. 11:20
we read of "the Lord's supper," and in Jude 12 a "love
feast" is mentioned. It was once supposed that these
terms were designations of different kinds of meals.
Today there is a tendency to regard them simply as
different names attached to the same thing; in each
case a particular aspect of a larger whole was selected
for emphasis. If so, the terms "breaking of bread"
and "Lord's supper" laid weight on participation in a
meal, while "love feast" stressed the fellowship of love
in the meal.

By the second and third centuries other names were
employed which had New Testament cognates or con-
notations. "Communion" was suggested by the reference
in I Cor. 10:16 to communion or participation in the
body and blood of Christ. "Eucharist" was suggested
by the giving of thanks (*eucharistein*) in connection
with the meal (Mark 14:23). Another name was "the

4

mystery." While this term was probably borrowed from a contemporary pagan designation for certain religious rites and ceremonies, it also reminded Christians of "the mysteries of God" (I Cor. 4:1). It was not always understood by them that in the New Testament "mystery" referred not to something secret and enigmatic but rather to something that had been hidden but was now revealed or made known; the revelation of God in Christ was the "mystery," and accordingly Paul could speak of "the mystery of the gospel" (Eph. 6:19). The misunderstanding was further compounded when the Greek word *mysterion* was translated into the Latin *sacramentum,* which meant "pledge," as in "pledge of allegiance." Our word "sacrament" came into being in this way, and the designation "Sacrament of the Altar" has been used to some extent since the fifth century.

Before this, by the end of the fourth century, the term "mass" was first attached to the Lord's Supper. It became the general designation in the West by the sixth century, and to this day it is still the word customarily used in the Roman Catholic Church. How deeply imbedded it became is illustrated by the fact that the English name for Christmas (Christ mass) is derived from it. The origin of the term is involved in some obscurity, but it seems probable that it came from the words of dismissal (missa = mass) which a priest used. Because it has a meaning which is not at all descriptive of the significance of what happens in the Lord's Supper, some Roman Catholics, like the French theologian Francois Amiot, deplore that the term supplanted earlier and better ones. Still other names employed need not detain us here.

In the first Anglican *Book of Common Prayer* (1549) we come upon the heading, "The Supper of the Lorde, and the Holy Communion, commonly called the Masse." Here three designations were brought together, and they were brought together in such a way as to indicate preference: what used to be called the Mass in the Middle Ages should henceforth, under the influence of the Reformation, once again be called the Lord's Supper, or (with reference to the restoration of the laity to full participation) may be called Holy Communion. Although the labels which were employed may be said to have no great importance in themselves, historically they came as a matter of fact to be significant indicators of different understandings of the sacrament.

VARIETY OF INTERPRETATION

Meals which were partly social and partly religious in character were not uncommon at the time when Jesus lived. Members of Greek and Roman guilds and associations often shared common meals. Such banquets are known to have been widely observed in Asia Minor, in Egypt, and in other lands into which Christianity first spread. Above all, religious-social meals were familiar to the Jews. In preparation for the Sabbath a weekly ceremony of eating and drinking, called a *kiddush,* was customary in Jewish homes. Sometimes small circles of friends also observed what they called a *chaburah,* a meal limited to a closely knit fellowship. Most familiar, however, was the passover feast which all Jews were expected to participate in once a year.

When Jesus met with his disciples in Jerusalem for the last time, therefore, we have no reason to suppose that there was anything at all unusual about their eating together. They must have done this often before. What made this last supper different from all other meals Jesus had eaten with his disciples was the special meaning he gave it. Whether in its essential features it actually was a passover or a *chaburah* or a *kiddush* has been much debated. However this may be, the Supper was afterwards generally interpreted with allusions to the passover.

The feast of the passover was for the Jews an annual

commemoration of Israel's escape from bondage in Egypt. A one-year-old male lamb without fault or blemish was ceremonially slaughtered by a priest and offered as a sacrifice that God might spare the people from the destroying angel who had slain the first-born of the Egyptians. The lamb was then roasted whole and was eaten by anywhere from ten to twenty persons, together with bitter herbs, unleavened bread, and wine.

Whether or not the Last Supper Jesus had with his disciples was in its outward form an anticipated passover feast, and whether a lamb or a kid was eaten there, the sacrificial lamb was afterwards understood by early Christians as a prefiguration of Jesus Christ, "the Lamb of God who takes away the sins of the world." In the accounts of the Last Supper Jesus himself spoke of his body which was about to be broken and of his blood which was about to be spilled. Thereafter the religious-social meals Christians continued to observe as a matter of course had a bright new meaning which they expressed in a variety of ways: they ate and drank "in remembrance" of him who had given himself in sacrifice for them on the cross; they were united with him who had made a "new covenant" with them and who was present among them as giver and gift; they received from him the "forgiveness of sins" and did "proclaim the Lord's death until he comes."

Down to our own day the Lord's Supper has been observed by almost all who have called themselves Christians. Quakers, Christian Scientists, and members of the Salvation Army are exceptions that prove the rule. But the rest have not always understood and interpreted their eating and drinking together in the same way. In very broad terms we can distinguish three major meanings which have been given to the Lord's Supper.

The first of these was an interpretation of the Lord's Supper in terms of sacrifice. This was not a farfetched notion, for not only Jews but also pagans in the ancient world offered sacrifices either as tokens of homage to God or as acts to secure God's favor. It was not altogether unnatural that some Christians, converted in the early centuries from Judaism or paganism, should carry such conceptions over with them into Christianity. That they did so is reflected in the sacrificial terminology increasingly employed with reference to the Lord's Supper after the second century. Such people thought of themselves as making an offering to God. The locution "Do this in remembrance of me" was interpreted as "Offer this in remembrance of me."

Such views were gradually developed by Ambrose in the fourth century, by Gregory the Great in the fifth century, by Paschasius Radbert in the ninth century, and by many others. In the course of the Middle Ages, in spite of protests by some theologians, decrees of councils strengthened an interpretation which had its roots in popular piety. The Fourth Lateran Council declared in 1215 that Christ's "body and blood are truly contained in the sacrament of the altar under the forms of bread and wine, the bread being changed into body and the wine into blood by divine power." This change of substances, called "transubstantiation," was said to be effected when a priest spoke the words, "This is my body," etc., over the elements. The fact that the elements retained their outward form, color, and taste

9

(technically called their "accidents") was explained by saying that the actual substances of bread and wine disappeared but their accidents remained. When, as occasionally happened, mice nibbled at the "transubstantiated" bread which had been laid aside, the question was raised as to whether it was really possible for mice to eat the accidents (that is, the form, color, and taste) of bread without its substance. Thomas Aquinas was more consistent than some others when he forthrightly answered that the mice ate the body of Christ.

Be this as it may, it was said that in a mass the priest who had changed the bread and wine into the substances of Christ's body and blood also offered these substances of the body and blood of Christ to God as a sacrifice for the sins of those people for whom he was saying mass. In 1562 the Council of Trent declared that "in this divine sacrifice which is celebrated in the mass, that same Christ, who once offered himself in a bloody manner on the altar of the cross, is contained and sacrificed in an unbloody manner. . . . This sacrifice is truly propitiatory." This is still the core of official Roman Catholic teaching today: in the mass a sacrifice is made by man to God for the purpose of securing God's favor. The direction of Eastern Orthodox and Anglo-Catholic interpretations is quite similar.

The second major interpretation of the Lord's Supper has been in terms of memorial rather than of sacrifice. It was denied, to begin with, that the bread and wine used in the sacrament were changed into the body and blood of Christ. The elements, it was said, are merely symbols of Christ's body which was broken and of his blood which was spilled. This view has also had a long history. There is evidence of this interpretation long before the fourth century, but in this and the following centuries preachers and theologians like Chrysostom gave it additional currency. It was more strongly and more exclusively asserted by such men as Rabanus Maurus in the ninth century and by Berengar of Tours in the eleventh century. It was taken up again in the sixteenth century by Ulrich Zwingli, whose name has especially been associated with it. "This is my body," he declared, means "This represents my body"—"just as a wife may say, 'This is my late husband,' when she shows her husband's ring."

More important than insistence that the elements in the sacrament are symbolical was the assertion that the fundamental purpose of the Lord's Supper is commemorative. Jesus Christ, wrote Zwingli, "instituted a remembrance of that deliverance by which he redeemed the whole world that we might never forget that for our sake he exposed his body to the ignominy of death—and not merely in order that we might not forget it in our hearts, but also that we might publicly attest it with praise and thanksgiving." Zwingli was fond of calling the Lord's Supper a "supper of thanksgiving" or "eucharist." It was thus considered a celebration of a past event, the death of Christ on the cross, and participants not only refreshed their memory of this event and its significance but also professed their faith before men. Such remains the meaning of the sacrament for adherents of some modern churches. Mennonites say that it "represents to us how Christ's holy body was sacrificed on the cross, . . . reminds us of the use of Christ's death, and exhorts us to love one another."

Baptists and others recognize in it a "mark of discipleship," and they prefer to call it an "ordinance" rather than a "sacrament" to make clear their difference from Roman Catholics. Yet, interestingly, this whole view resembles the Catholic position in one important respect: the emphasis is on what man does. For Catholics, man offers a sacrifice to God; for these others, man reminds himself of Christ's sacrifice on the cross, gives thanks for it, and publicly identifies himself as a Christian.

The third major interpretation of the Lord's Supper has been in terms of what God does and gives rather than in terms of what man does either by way of offering a sacrifice or by way of celebrating a memorial. Among others, Augustine in the fifth century and Pierre d'Ailly in the fifteenth dismissed the notion that in the sacrament bread and wine are changed into the body and blood of Christ. The theory of transubstantiation is "a monstrous word for a monstrous idea," Martin Luther wrote later. "It is an absurd and unheard-of juggling with words." The bread remains bread, as the wine remains wine. "That bread is and remains there agrees better with the Scriptures, as St. Paul himself states, 'The bread which we break' (I Cor. 10:16)." This does not mean, however, that the bread and wine are *merely* symbols in the context of the Lord's Supper. To be sure, they are symbols, too, but Christ himself (not simply metaphysical substances of his body and blood)—he who became incarnate and gave his body to be broken and his blood to be spilled for us—is present "in the whole action or transaction" when people assemble to eat and drink in keeping with his institution and promise.

According to this third interpretation, the Lord's Supper must be understood in the light of what happened on the cross for us and for our salvation. "The forgiveness of sins, life, and salvation are given to us in the sacrament," Luther wrote in his *Small Catechism*. The "chief thing in the sacrament" is what God has done and continues to do in Christ, not what man does. In popular terminology, it is a sacrament and not a sacrifice. The Augsburg Confession therefore declared that "the sacraments were instituted not only to be signs by which people might be identified outwardly as Christians, but they are signs and testimonies of God's will toward us." In similar vein John Calvin wrote in his *Institutes* that a sacrament is "a testimony of the grace of God toward us, confirmed by an outward sign, with a reciprocal attestation of our piety toward him." Making allowance for differences which exist, this has been the position of Lutherans, Presbyterians, the Reformed, Methodists, and also those Anglicans who have not, under the influence of the Oxford Movement, receded to the first interpretation described above.

This brief sketch of three interpretations of the Lord's Supper does not do justice to all the nuances which actually appear, but it will serve as a rough frame of reference within which shades of meaning and varieties of practice can conveniently be described. When the three interpretations are designated as sacrificial, commemorative, and sacramental, these labels are simply intended to indicate the major directions.

Meanwhile it will be noticed that each of these interpretations points in one way or another to the sacrifice of Christ on the cross. The first understands the sacrament as either a repetition or a re-presentation to God of Christ's sacrifice. The second understands it as a remembrance of the sacrifice which is altogether in the past. The third understands it as a present giving to men of all that was won by Christ in his once-for-all sacrifice on the cross.

AGAPE OR LOVE FEAST

The accounts which have come down to us of the last meeting our Lord had with his disciples "on the night when he was betrayed" indicate that a meal, a "supper," was eaten. After the crucifixion and resurrection those who were called Christians continued to meet, and in their assemblies "they partook of food with glad and generous hearts, praising God" (Acts 2:46-47). Such meals in which rich and poor, masters and slaves ate together were expressions of Christian joy, unity, and brotherhood. They also provided a handy way of extending charity to the poor and needy, who were given food and drink out of the supplies brought by those who were able. The choice of some men to "serve tables" (Acts 6:1-2) appears to have reference to suppers of this sort which were part of the public worship, culminating in what we today call the sacrament, of the first Christians. The name "love feast" (Jude 12) was sometimes applied to them.

Fuller accounts of such banquets or feasts have come down to us from the centuries immediately following the apostolic age. In addition to bread and wine (the staple food and drink of the time), meat, poultry, fish, cheese, honey, and milk were often served. At the very close of the second century Tertullian wrote:

> Our feast explains itself by its name. The Greeks call it *agape*, which means "love." Whatever it costs,

15

our outlay in the name of piety is gain, for with the good things of the feast we benefit the needy. . . . As it is an act of religious service, . . . the participants, before reclining, taste first of prayer to God. As much is eaten as satisfies the cravings of hunger; as much is drunk as befits the sober. . . . We talk as persons who know that the Lord is one of our auditors. . . . We are prompted to stand forth and sing, as we can, a hymn to God. . . . As the feast commenced with prayer, so with prayer it is closed.

By the time Tertullian wrote these words, what we call the Lord's Supper had begun to be separated from the *agape* or love feast of which it had earlier been a part. It is not difficult to imagine how radically this changed the atmosphere in which the sacrament was celebrated. Several factors played a part in the separation. Paul had already complained about abuses which had appeared among the Christians in Corinth. The rich ate and drank immoderately and without waiting for the poor and the slaves to come from their work, with the result that the latter sometimes remained hungry, and brotherly fellowship was destroyed (I Cor. 11:17-22). Elsewhere, too, social distinctions seem to have reasserted themselves as Christian communities grew. Moreover, love feasts became objects of criticism from the outside when pagans and even government officials misunderstood or misrepresented their significance. Still later, when churches were built, some questioned the propriety of serving meals in these buildings, although there is no evidence that questions had been raised before about doing this in the houses and other halls in which Christians had been meeting. Of course, there were also practical problems connected with serving meals when congregations grew in membership.

The divorce of the sacrament from the love feast did not mean that the latter was abandoned at once. On the contrary, love feasts continued to be held as expressions of Christian joy and fellowship and as vehicles for charitable work. They also continued to be intimately associated with worship. But the reasons which led to their separation from the sacrament ultimately led to their suppression. In the course of the fourth century several councils of the church prohibited their further observance. However, the fact that the Council of Trullo had to repeat the prohibition of love feasts as late as A.D. 692 suggests that many were reluctant to abandon them. Actually remnants of love feasts persisted long afterwards in the distribution of bread and wine to the poor in medieval churches.

Love feasts have enjoyed a limited revival in modern times. In the summer of 1727 a group of Moravians in Saxony, after participating in the Lord's Supper, paused outside their meeting place to talk about the blessings they had just received and to express their joy by singing hymns. Observing this, their spiritual leader Count Nicholas von Zinzendorf had some food and drink brought to them. Afterwards he reflected on the similarity of this spontaneous refreshment to the primitive *agape*. Ever since that time, in addition to their observances of the Lord's Supper, most Moravians have held love feasts in their churches to cultivate their fellowship, equality, and unity with one another in Christ. In a special service of song and prayer, an address occasionally being added, simple refreshments are served. In Europe tea and currant buns are usually provided; in America coffee and cake are more customary, although lemonade and hot chocolate are sometimes used. Men carry mugs of the beverage on trays down the aisles to the pews in which the people are seated, and women, often wearing little white caps brought from Moravia, distribute the cake in similar fashion. The following lines of a hymn reflect the spirit of the Moravian love feast:

> Lord Jesus, for our call of grace,
> To praise thy name in fellowship,
> We're humbly met before thy face
> And in thy presence love-feast keep.

From the Moravians the early Methodists borrowed the observance of love feasts. John Wesley, the father of the Methodist awakening, reported in 1748:

> I desired that . . . we might together "eat bread," as the ancient Christians did, "with gladness and singleness of heart." At these love feasts (so we termed them, retaining the name as well as the thing which was in use from the beginning) our food is only a little plain cake and water. But we seldom return from them without being fed not only with the "meat which perisheth" but with "that which endureth to everlasting life."

Such Methodist love feasts, which became occasions for "testimonies" to one another of experiences of faith and love, were observed until the middle of the nineteenth century.

Other revivals occurred among smaller religious bodies. The Brethren, popularly called "Dunkers" in North America because they baptized by immersion, observed what they called a "feast of charity." Preceded by the rite of footwashing, this evening meal consisted of soup, meat, potatoes, and vegetables, and it was followed by the consumption of unleavened bread and wine. Similar was the practice of the Sandemanians, a small sect founded by a former Scottish Presbyterian minister in the eighteenth century, except that Scotch broth was used. The celibate members of the short-lived Ephrata Community, established in Pennsylvania about the same time, also had love feasts. So did the Amana Society, which in 1855 founded a religious community in Iowa and did not abandon its communal life until 1932. In the Peace Mission Movement, an eccentric cult which flourished in America especially during the great economic depression of the 1930's, "Father Divine" presided regularly at an elaborate banquet called "God's Holy Communion."

After World War II an attempt was made under the influence of the ecumenical movement to bridge the gulf between churches in local communities. An Anglican parish and a Methodist congregation in Norfolk, England, experimented with a union service which featured a love feast. Since ecclesiastical and other differences prevented a joint celebration of the Lord's Supper, it was decided to begin with a restoration of the primitive *agape* in the simple form in which Moravians observed it. Although this interdenominational love feast was repeated in Norfolk, it did not result in wider use.

However, whenever congregational dinners are held today for the purpose of cultivating fellowship among members, at least one of the functions of the early Christian love feast may be realized. The same may even be true of the practice, observed in some churches today, of serving coffee and cake after a service. On the other hand, changing conditions and expanding needs have long since led to the adoption of more effective means to express charitable impulses, although these still have a place in the public worship of churches today wherever offerings are gathered for works of mercy. In the case of the love feast, at all events, we can see how a practice of the primitive church has in the course of time undergone a variety of adaptations and, except for isolated attempts at restoration, has virtually disappeared.

BREAD AND WINE

Although, as we have observed, many other forms of food were eaten in the early church in connection with the Lord's Supper, from the beginning bread was always eaten. If the Last Supper in Jerusalem was a passover feast, unleavened bread would have been used, but it is not at all certain that this was the case. What is known of early observances of the Lord's Supper suggests that what was used was the bread ordinarily eaten by the people, not a special kind of bread. Loaves of leavened bread were brought to the assemblies of Christians, and pieces were broken from the loaves to distribute among the people.

By the ninth century unleavened bread began to be substituted for leavened bread in the West. Originally the reason for this change was undoubtedly a practical concern to prevent the bread, when it was laid aside for a time, from becoming moldy and spoiling. Another reason was soon added when the church wanted to suggest that the bread used in the Mass was not ordinary bread after all. In time this impression was reinforced by reducing the size of the bread from a loaf to a small roll and then to a thin wafer, and this had a further practical advantage, for the bite-sized wafers did not need to be broken from a larger loaf or roll for distribution.

In the East the older practice of using leavened bread

was retained, and in the eleventh century, after heated debates as to the proper form, it was agreed in the West as well as in the East that either leavened or unleavened bread might be employed. However, the Eastern Orthodox clung to their practice and to this day use leavened bread. On the other hand, Roman Catholics in the West insisted on the exclusive use of wafers, and today a Roman Catholic priest who employs any other form of bread is declared guilty of mortal sin.

Both in the East and in the West rigid regulations prescribed exactly how the bread was to be prepared. In the thirteenth century, for example, the Bishop of Lincoln, in England, wrote to the priests under his jurisdiction that more than ordinary care must be taken that wafers be baked out of pure wheat flour and water, without adding oil or fat, and that during their preparation a priest must be present and must be vested in his cassock and surplice. When the dough was ready it was placed between two heated iron plates in which were engraved figures of a lamb, of the crucifixion, of a cross, or such symbols as AO ("I am the Alpha and the Omega" [Rev. 1:8]) or IHS (the first Greek letters of the name "Jesus"). Between the heated plates, much as in a modern waffle iron, the wafers were quickly baked and were in the process stamped with the selected figures or symbols. In the Middle Ages the name "host" (from the Latin *hostia,* meaning sacrifice) was given to these wafers because it was believed that they were changed by priests into the body of Christ and sacrificed to God.

That such wafers were often made in church buildings is attested by the survival of ovens, and long after the

Reformation "yrons for prynted caks" are mentioned in the inventories of Protestant ministers as well as Roman Catholic priests both in Europe and in America. At the time of the Reformation neither Lutherans nor Anglicans evinced any interest in altering the form of the bread again, so wafers continued to be used. The first *Book of Common Prayer* provided that the bread should be "unleavened and round, as it was afore, but without all manner of print." This did not satisfy the Puritans in England any more than the retention of wafers by Lutherans on the continent pleased the Reformed. Those who came to be called Presbyterians, Congregationalists, and Baptists as well as the Reformed insisted on returning to the more ancient use of ordinary bread, thus avoiding the "popish" innovation of the Middle Ages. Instead of breaking pieces from a whole loaf, however, they cut slices into small cubes before the observance of the Lord's Supper.

In the seventeenth century, when party feeling was unusually bitter and the kind of bread employed became a bone of contention, the Lutheran theologian John Andrew Quenstedt complained that the Reformed ridiculed the "foam-like bread," the "small pieces of paste," and the "little paper cakes" which the Lutherans used. He conceded, however, that the quality, quantity, and outward form of the bread did not matter, provided only it was of the substance of bread. If, he added, there is a place somewhere in the world so barbarous that no grain is available for the making of bread, Christians should engage in agriculture so that bread may be had. A contemporary of Quenstedt, Frederick Balduin, reported that there were parts of India in which grain would not grow. In such regions, he suggested, Christians might substitute what they regularly ate in place of bread. Such problems are more hypothetical than real today when leavened bread or unleavened wafers (or even soda crackers, which the Jehovah's Witnesses prefer to use) are commercially manufactured and distributed.

As bread was the staple food at the time of Jesus, so wine was the common drink. There can be no doubt that Jesus used red wine at the institution of the Lord's Supper and that such wine was generally used in the sacrament for centuries afterwards. However, there were some Christians in the early centuries who substituted water, either because they ascribed importance only to the bread or because they had an aversion to wine. Others used juice freshly pressed from grapes or, for want of grapes, made a beverage from raisins. As a rule water was mingled with the wine because people were then accustomed to dilute their wine to make it more palatable when they drank it in everyday use. Only later was this carry-over from ordinary drinking customs embroidered with allegorical meanings. In the fourth century, for example, Ambrose suggested that the mingling of water with wine in the sacrament signified the water which issued with blood from our Lord's side when he was hanging on the cross, and others saw in this usage a proof of the union of the human and divine natures in Christ.

When Christianity extended its influence beyond the lands bordering on the Mediterranean Sea, it gained adherents in places where there were no vineyards and where wine was not the staple drink of the people. In

England, for example, mead (somewhat akin to ale or beer) was the common drink, and because wine had to be imported it was scarce and expensive. Under these circumstances the common beverage made out of grain was occasionally substituted for "the fruit of the vine." This solution was generally repudiated, and in 1567 a minister of the Church of England was suspended from office when he "indede did minister the communion with beare, but it was onelie for necessitie and want of wyne."

Another attempt to meet the problem occasioned by shortage of wine was to dip part of the wafer in wine and distribute it to the people in this moistened condition. The practice of "intinction," as this was called, became the common practice in the East, where the bread, dipped in wine, was placed directly into the mouth of the communicant on a spoon. In the West, however, intinction was opposed and finally prohibited long before the Reformation. On the one hand, it was said, it is contrary to the institution of the sacrament and to its symbolical significance to administer the elements together instead of separately. On the other hand, intinction suggested the sop of Judas referred to in John 13:26, 27, "So when he had dipped the morsel [in the Latin Vulgate, *intinctum panem*], he gave it to Judas, . . . [and] Satan entered into him." Rather than substitute another liquid for wine and rather than moisten the bread with a little wine, the problem of wine-shortage was met in the late Middle Ages by administering only bread to the laity and by saying that it was enough for the priest to drink wine in behalf of the people. Other factors also played a part in the decision to withhold the chalice from the laity, as we shall see, but this was one of them.

In the late Middle Ages and afterwards there was also some question as to the color of wine that ought to be used. It was argued that red wine should be retained because of tradition, and also because a near-sighted priest might have difficulty in distinguishing white wine from water. On the other hand, it was argued that, if by accident it was spilled, white wine would not stain altar cloths and vestments as red wine would. No binding regulation was made concerning the color of wine, but since the Reformation Roman Catholics have tended to prefer white wine and the Eastern Orthodox to prefer red wine. Protestants have showed a preference for red sacramental wine, which had been customary before the Reformation, and as a rule they do not mingle water with the wine.

Throughout the history of the church there were cases of individuals who could not tolerate wine on their stomachs. This ceased to be a problem for Roman Catholics after the withholding of the cup from the laity, but it continued to be a problem for Protestants who insisted that the sacrament requires the use of wine as well as bread on the part of all participants. In the seventeenth century the Lutheran theologian John Gerhard advised that individuals who could not tolerate wine should refrain from participating in the Lord's Supper altogether inasmuch as man's relation to God is established and nourished in other ways as well as by means of the sacrament, and he cited the saying of Augustine, "Believe and you have eaten." On the other hand, Protestants in the Calvinistic tradition were more ready to substitute another liquid for wine in such instances. Consequently English missionaries in South Africa, for example, had no compunctions about using banana juice in place of wine.

When in the course of the nineteenth century a movement to abolish all manufacture and use of alcoholic beverages gained strength especially in America and Great Britain, there was growing reluctance to continue to use wine in the Lord's Supper. It was even suggested, although without foundation, that the "wine" employed by Jesus at the institution of the Lord's Supper must have been unfermented juice of grapes. In any case grape juice began to be substituted for wine, and this practice was accelerated when in the latter half of the nineteenth century a process was developed commercially for the preservation and distribution of bottled grape juice. The use of grape juice became quite general among Methodists, Baptists, Presbyterians, Congregationalists, and others in North America, and from America its use spread, although in a much more limited way, to Europe and to mission fields elsewhere in the world.

Some Lutherans in America were moved by similar concerns to borrow the practice from their neighbors, but generally, both here and abroad, they adhered to the earlier custom of employing wine. However, in the case of alcoholics who might be tempted by drinking sacramental wine to return to excessive use of alcohol, Lutherans in Europe as well as in America have not hesitated in recent years to substitute grape juice for wine.

Even with respect to the elements used in the Lord's Supper, therefore, new times and circumstances have in-

27

troduced, and are still introducing, changes, and to some extent these changes have been colored by different understandings of the sacrament.

BLESSING OR CONSECRATION

When Jews engaged in their religious-social meals it was customary for somebody to "bless" the bread and wine before eating and drinking. The form of blessing was invariable: "Blessed art thou, O Lord, who bringest forth bread from the earth, . . . who dost create the fruit of the vine." It was deemed a sacrilege to partake of food and drink without thanking God for his gifts. As the words indicate, it was not the food and drink that were blessed but it was God who was blessed, and "to bless God" meant to thank him, to acknowledge his gifts with gratitude. This is what our Lord did on the night when he was betrayed: he "took bread, and *when he had given thanks,* he broke it, and gave it to the disciples. . . . In the same way also he took the cup, and *when he had given thanks* he gave it to them. . . ."

By the second, third, and fourth centuries this was no longer understood by some converts from paganism. They saw in such blessing something analogous to pagan incantations to which they had been accustomed. They believed that the elements ceased to be "profane" and became "holy" when a prayer was said over them or the words of institution were recited. That this was by no means the universal belief is attested, for example, by *The Testament of our Lord,* a fifth-century church order, which contains a prayer that the bread and wine may benefit the communicants without the slightest suggestion that anything at all happens to the elements.

After the fourth century, however, the notion that the bread and wine were changed became more and more common. In the East it expressed itself in the *epiklesis,* a special prayer invoking God to cause his Spirit to descend on the bread and wine and change these into the body and blood of Christ: "We pray, beg, and beseech thee to send down thy Holy Spirit . . . upon these gifts here present; make this bread the sacred body of thy Christ, and make what is in this chalice the precious blood of thy Christ, changing them by thy Holy Spirit." In the West, on the other hand, the same change was believed to take place on the strength of a priest's act of *consecration* by his use of the words of institution. At the very moment a priest, taking the bread, uttered the words, "This is my body," and at the very moment he, taking the wine, uttered the words, "This is the chalice of my blood," the substances of these elements were said to be changed into Christ's body and blood. To this day the Eastern Orthodox believe that a change in the elements is effected through the *epiklesis,* and Roman Catholics believe that the same change is accomplished by consecration.

Such beliefs were inevitably reflected in rites and ceremonies. In the twelfth century priests in the West marked the "moment" of the appearance and sacrifice of Christ's body by genuflecting before and adoring the host which had just been consecrated. The bread was then lifted up so that the people might "see God," as it was put. This "elevation" of the host was accompanied by the ringing of a sanctus bell or sacring bell ("sacring" is an archaic form of the word "consecrating"). The attention of the people was thus called to what was alleged to be happening at the altar, and they, too, fell upon their knees to adore the body of Christ under the form of bread. This whole procedure was repeated in connection with the consecration of the wine, but it was deemed especially meaningful in the case of the bread because, according to the theory of sacramental concomitance, the blood as well as the body of Christ were in the bread alone.

Incense came to be used here as elsewhere. In ancient times incense had often been used by pagans in connection with their sacrifices, and because of this association Christians refrained for centuries from using it in their worship. Their aversion to the use of incense was gradually overcome, and it was used for the very practical purpose of disguising offensive odors in church buildings. By the ninth century its use was given ceremonial significance. Thomas Aquinas wrote four centuries later that incense was used primarily for purposes of fumigation, and secondarily to represent symbolically the ascent of prayer or the sweet savor of divine grace. Now incense, smoking in a portable container called a thurible, was also swung in the direction of persons or things to show honor or homage. Not only the priests ministering at an altar but also the altar itself and the elements of bread and wine were "censed" as if to insure their "holiness." At the same time the sign of the cross was made over the elements—a total of twenty times—as a supplementary blessing or consecration.

Great care was exercised to prevent the wine, which was believed to have been changed into the actual blood of Christ by means of consecration, from spilling. One

31

of the reasons for withholding the cup from the laity was to avoid this desecration, for it was difficult if not impossible to prevent spilling some wine during its distribution to large numbers of communicants. So the priests alone consumed the consecrated wine. Even they were required to take precautions, however, lest the blood of Christ be profaned. After the chalice had been drained, the priest poured fresh water and wine into it, and with this he rinsed the chalice, his mouth, and his fingers "lest any remains of the body or blood cling to his fingers or to the chalice," a late medieval rubric specified.

Similar precautions were observed with respect to the bread. The use of wafers commended itself over the use of loaves from which pieces were broken because crumbs were less likely to fall to the ground. Since it was still possible to drop a wafer or part of one while distributing bread to the laity, however, cloths were held under the chins of communicants to protect against accidents. Moreover, instead of placing the host in the hands of communicants, as had been customary earlier, the bread was now placed directly in their mouths. All such practices underscored the belief that as a result of consecration the elements were no longer bread and wine but had become the body and blood of Christ.

Since only a small quantity of wine was employed and all of the consecrated wine was normally consumed at once, there was no problem in the Middle Ages about the treatment of the wine left over. But since the number of lay communicants varied from time to time, there could be a surplus of consecrated wafers. These were the body of Christ, it was taught, and they remained so until they were digested or otherwise destroyed. The wafers were therefore treated accordingly. They were placed in a receptacle (a ciborium), shaped like a chalice with a lid, and this receptacle was in turn housed in a more or less elaborate "tabernacle" resting on the altar, or, more rarely, the wafers were kept in a pyx, or box, suspended above the altar. A perpetual light, or sanctuary lamp, was placed before the tabernacle or pyx to mark the presence of the body of Christ there under the form of bread. The reserved host was an object of worship itself, and it was displayed for this purpose.

All the practices just described were rooted in a conception of priestly consecration very different from the "blessing" for bread and wine in the primitive church. The Protestant Reformers called attention to this. Although some of them retained the term "consecration," they made it clear that they no longer meant the same thing by it. They spoke therefore of "the words of institution, which used to be called words of consecration," or "the words of blessing or consecration." In these words, the Reformers declared, God addressed men directly and personally; the words were in no sense addressed to the bread and wine, nor did they change these elements. They were accordingly no longer to be whispered by the priest as had become customary; they were to be spoken in a loud, clear voice, and no longer in Latin but in the language the people could understand. Of course, the very fact that the Reformers uniformly rejected any theory of transubstantiation or impanation (proposed by William of Ockham) or con-substantiation (repudiated by Lutherans when ascribed

33

to them) in itself also implied a rejection of what had come to be called consecration.

It took a long time, however, before the people rid themselves of conceptions and practices long associated with the Mass. Early in his career Luther wrote with reference to the sacrifice of the Mass:

> I am attacking a difficult matter, an abuse perhaps impossible to uproot, since through century-long custom and the common consent of men it has become so firmly entrenched that it would be necessary to abolish most of the books now in vogue, to alter almost the entire external form of the churches, and to introduce, or rather re-introduce, a totally different kind of ceremonies.

Luther was more conservative and more patient than most of the other Reformers. He was willing, "chiefly on account of the weak in faith, who might be greatly offended by a sudden change," to postpone changes in practice which a changed understanding of the sacrament demanded. He and his colleagues began with those practices which could no longer be "observed without sin" because they were "contrary to the gospel." From this initially negative approach they and their successors proceeded to more positive attempts to create forms which expressed or exhibited what they believed happened in the sacrament.

Gradually observances rooted in a conception of priestly consecration were altered or abandoned. The elevation of the elements, the ringing of the sacring bell, and the genuflection of minister and people were discontinued. The censing of bread and wine and the use of the sign of the cross over them fell into disuse. Meticulous precautions to prevent the spilling of wine and the dropping of bread ceased to have meaning, and so the ceremonial rinsing of fingers and chalice and the use of a cloth to catch fragments of bread which might accidentally fall disappeared. Often the bread once again was placed in the hands of communicants instead of into their mouths. The reservation of bread on the altar or elsewhere and the adoration of this bread as if it were actually the body of Christ were forbidden, and sanctuary lamps which had been associated with reservation were removed from churches.

Here and there, under the influence of Romanticism, there were Protestant revivals of some of these practices, especially in the nineteenth century and again more recently. The motivation was usually esthetic or antiquarian, although a conscious or unconscious return to a sub-Christian conception of consecration has not been entirely wanting. An instance of this may be seen in the occasional practice of "reconsecrating" bread and wine when the supply of these elements is exhausted during administration. This can hardly mean anything else than a belief that words spoken over bread and wine change these elements in some way. This belief and this practice cannot be harmonized with the blessing or thanksgiving of the primitive observance of the Lord's Supper.

Such forms and practices which have recently been introduced into some Protestant churches stand in sharp contradiction not only to the New Testament understanding of blessing but also to the official teachings of these churches themselves. People are likely to be con-

35

fused when the witness of a congregation is obscured by its practice. This is to be deplored especially in a time like ours when widespread religious illiteracy demands the utmost clarity and the strictest adherence to reality and truth.

MINISTRANTS AND ALTARS

The New Testament does not tell us by whom the Lord's Supper was administered in the primitive church. In the course of the second and third centuries we encounter evidence of a belief that the administration of the sacrament required special officiants. Some held that these were necessary merely for the sake of good order, and others implied that they were essential to the very efficacy of the act.

The latter view gradually prevailed, and those who presided at the Lord's Supper were called "priests" who made "sacrifices" to God. This had the effect of so shifting the emphasis in the Lord's Supper that Thomas Aquinas could write in the thirteenth century: "the perfection of this sacrament is not in its use by the faithful but in the consecration of the elements" by a priest. Now it was asserted that by virtue of his ordination a power was conferred on a priest to enable him, and him alone, to transubstantiate bread and wine into the body and blood of Christ and offer these to God as a propitiatory sacrifice. The dignity of the priest was further exalted by the withdrawal of the cup from the laity and by the claim that the priest drinks from the chalice "not for himself only but for all the faithful." To this day when a man is ordained as a priest in the Roman Catholic church he is presented with a chalice to symbolize the unique power, believed to be conferred on him, to offer the sacrifice of the Mass.

During the Reformation some extremists reacted so violently against what they looked upon as the arrogant presumption of priests that they were reluctant to acknowledge any office at all in the church. Quakers and Plymouth Brethren represent this sharp rejection down to our own day. However, most of the Reformers declared that the very nature of the Word of God (a message to be proclaimed) and of the sacraments (acts to be performed) demand preachers, teachers, ministrants. A ministry was therefore to be retained to carry out a necessary function. Ministers were selected or called for this purpose by the church, and ordination, with prayer and the laying on of hands, was regarded as a public attestation of this call rather than as a bestowal on the ordinand of an "indelible character" which empowered him to do what a layman could not do. To employ the language of the Reformation, the ministry was an office and not an order.

What this meant with reference to the Lord's Supper was that in theory a layman could administer the sacrament without in any way diminishing its validity or efficacy. In practice, however, this was exceptional. For the sake of good order laymen administered only where formally ordained ministers were not available. Even in such emergency situations a layman who administered the sacrament was "called" to do so by the consent of the people who participated, and this underscored the fundamental Protestant position that the ministry is the exercise of a function which belongs to the church and not merely to a special class or order of men.

In early times the Lord's Supper appears to have been administered as a rule in private homes in which Christians were accustomed to assemble. Only when and where their numbers made it feasible were special buildings erected. In the fourth century, when persecutions ceased and Christianity began to enjoy the favor of civil authorities, churches were built in large numbers. Regulations were then adopted to forbid observance of the Lord's Supper outside of church buildings, except for the benefit of the sick. It is still the Roman Catholic rule that Mass may not be said, except under special circumstances, outside of a church, and such a building must first be "consecrated" by sprinkling parts of it with holy water, censing other parts of it, and anointing still other parts with oil.

Concurrent with this development was the substitution of altars for the tables which had earlier been used for the administration of the sacrament. There is no doubt that non-Christian influences, notably the growth of sacrificial notions, contributed to this change, but concern for orderly administration in the expanding congregations also played a part. Early altars, like the earlier tables, were made of wood, but stone altars soon appeared, and by the sixth century we find legislation requiring the use of stone. Afterwards symbolical meaning was attached to the materials used, and it was said that a stone altar signifies the rock of salvation.

During the Reformation there were objections to the continued use of altars on the ground that they were associated with the Roman sacrifice of the Mass. In 1550 all altars in the Church of England were ordered removed and replaced with tables in order "to turn the simple from the old superstitious opinions of the popish mass." Similar changes were introduced in Reformed and Presbyterian, in Congregational and Baptist churches. Although tables supplanted altars in some Lutheran churches, for the most part Lutherans allowed the altars to remain in the buildings they had inherited from the Middle Ages. They tried to make it clear, however, that they did not keep them as places of sacrifice either "in the sense of the Levitical law" or in the sense of the Roman Mass. Under the influence of Romanticism in the nineteenth century, altars were restored in many Anglican churches, and more recently the same has happened even in a few churches of the Calvinistic tradition.

In the early centuries of the Christian era a church had only one table or altar, but in the course of the Middle Ages it became common in the West for a church to have many altars—one "high" altar and several "side" altars. The multiplication of altars resulted from a multiplication of masses, and this in turn was a consequence of the notion, widely held since the sixth century, that by "offering the sacrifice of the Mass" special favors could be secured from God. "Mass priests" made their living from the fees people paid to have masses said for protection against diseases or bad weather, for safety when entering upon a journey, for success in a business venture, for happiness in marriage. In rural areas priests were asked to say masses for the safe delivery of cows, ewes, or mares. The sixteenth-century English poet Burnaby Googe put into verse some of the benefits which were believed, and still are believed, to result from "votive masses" or masses for special intentions:

Mass doth defend the traveller from danger and disease;
Mass doth preserve the sailing ship amid the raging seas.
Mass giveth store of corn and grain, and helpeth husbandry;
Mass blesseth every such as seeks in wealthy state to be.
Mass gets a man a pleasant wife, and gets the maid her mate;
Mass helps the captain in the field, and furthereth debate. . . .

A Roman Catholic priest recently described such votive masses as "eminently Catholic." The Protestant Reformers uniformly condemned them as a complete distortion of the Lord's Supper. "This notion has taken hold among the people and has infinitely multiplied the masses," the Apology of the Augsburg Confession asserted. "Masses are sold as the price for success, to merchants for good business, to hunters for good hunting. . . . They cannot produce a syllable from the Scriptures in support of the fairy tales which they teach so authoritatively in the church; nor do they have the support of the ancient church and the Fathers." All Protestants repudiated the claims of the Roman church, some of them because they interpreted the sacrament as a symbolical profession of their faith, but most of them because they interpreted the sacrament in terms of God's address to man in judgment and grace rather than in terms of man's approach to God with a sacrifice to secure his favor. In either case they discontinued nuptial masses, requiem masses (for the dead in purgatory), and other votive masses. In so doing they sharply reduced the frequency of public observances, and all altars except one could be removed from the churches in which Protestants worshiped.

PREPARATION AND RECEPTION

Participation in the Lord's Supper was from early times reserved for the intimate fellowship of Christians. Non-Christians were excluded. Members of early communities who were under discipline because of either betrayal of faith or moral lapses were also refused access to the sacrament, at least for a time. They were said to be "excommunicated," and this meant that they were banned from the fellowship and from communion with and in the fellowship until they gave sufficient evidence of repentance to be restored. Just what constituted evidence of repentance, and who was to judge this, was much debated in early centuries.

Whether children participated in the Lord's Supper with their parents during the first centuries cannot be determined with certainty for want of evidence, but it is unlikely. Whatever may have been the case earlier, by the fourth century it had become quite common for children to be admitted to the Lord's Supper directly after their baptism. With the introduction in the early Middle Ages of a separate rite of confirmation, reception of communion followed directly upon confirmation. The Council of Cologne (1280) forbade confirmation of children before the age of seven years, and it became the custom at the close of the Middle Ages, and it has remained the custom in the Roman Catholic church, for children to "make their first communion" at about the age of seven. At this time, it was said, they reach the "years of discretion."

Behind the church's long uncertainty about admitting children to the Lord's Supper was a debate about the necessity of the sacrament for salvation. Those who argued for early communion did so on the ground that only through reception of the body and blood of Christ could a child be "incorporated in Christ" and have a right to enter heaven. Those, on the other hand, who argued for postponement of communion did so on the ground that a child was already "incorporated in Christ" through baptism and that participation in the Lord's Supper was not necessary for salvation. This is the view that prevailed, and in 1562 the Council of Trent finally settled the question for Roman Catholics by decreeing, "If anyone says that the communion of the eucharist is necessary for little children before they have arrived at years of discretion, let him be anathema."

Protestants did not find fault with the substance of this conclusion, but after following the Roman practice for a short time they postponed confirmation or its equivalent, and hence also admission to the Lord's Supper, to about the twelfth to fourteenth year. They were encouraged to do so by the seriousness with which they took the apostolic injunction, "Let a man examine himself, . . . for anyone who eats and drinks without discerning the body eats and drinks judgment upon himself" (I Cor. 11:28-29).

In addition to self-examination other forms of preparation for communion had become customary. By the close of the fourth century fasting was recommended, and a number of councils of the church in this and in succeeding centuries required it of the clergy. By the ninth century laymen, too, were required to fast before communion. It was said that "the body of the Lord should enter the mouth of a Christian before other food." The implication was that the bread used in the sacrament was no longer bread and that it would be dishonored by receiving it in one's stomach on top of ordinary food. The requirement of fasting was soon defined to mean that ordinary food and drink should not be consumed between midnight and one's reception of the host the following morning. In general this remains the Roman Catholic rule today, and for the scrupulous it is explained that the fast is not broken by inadvertently swallowing tobacco dust or smoke, toothpaste, or particles of food from the previous day which had become lodged between the teeth.

A Roman Catholic who broke his fast in the eighteenth century is reported to have defended himself by saying that it is more respectful to receive the host on top of food than to put food on top of the host. The logic of this is recognized to a degree by Catholic casuists who recommend that one should wait a decent interval after communion before eating, and also that one should, if at all possible, avoid spitting for some time afterwards.

It seemed strange to the Protestant Reformers that "ordinary food," which is God's creation and his gift to man, should be thus deprecated. It also seemed strange to them that Christ himself, the disciples, and the early Christians should have received the sacrament "after supper" if worthy reception demanded fasting. Luther's totally different orientation is expressed in his *Small*

Catechism: "Fasting and bodily preparation are a good external discipline, but he is truly worthy and well prepared who believes these words: 'given for you' and 'for the forgiveness of sins.'" The difference between Catholics and Protestants on this matter is obviously related to the difference in their whole interpretation of the sacrament.

The same is true to a lesser degree with regard to the posture of communicants. At the institution, and in the early church generally, it is probable that participants in the Supper either reclined or sat at table, for one or the other of these positions was then customary. Then for several centuries, when the larger number of Christians made it inconvenient to sit at table, they stood for reception of communion. In their eyes standing was the posture for rejoicing, kneeling the posture for penitence. The Eastern Orthodox have preserved the custom of standing to our own day. On the other hand, it became customary in the West during the Middle Ages to kneel rather than stand for reception of communion. Whatever the origin of the change may have been, it was well suited to the adoration increasingly directed toward the consecrated elements. During the Reformation, at all events, when Anglicans continued the practice of kneeling at reception of the elements it was felt necessary to add the caution: "Thereby no adoration is intended, or ought to be done, . . . for that were idolatry." Methodists later followed Anglican practice. Lutherans also continued the inherited practice of kneeling in many places, although some Lutherans stood and others walked around the altar to receive first bread and then wine. The Dutch and German Reformed stood so as to avoid the suspicion of idolatry.

It was in the British Isles that the posture of communicants was most hotly debated in the sixteenth and seventeenth centuries. English law required kneeling in the established church, but many Calvinist-oriented ministers and lay people called Puritans had scruples lest by kneeling they "commyt idolitrie." One layman declared that he would rather hazard all the land he had than be drawn to kneel at communion. When in a sermon a minister was reported to have said "that our Lord Christ ministered the hoolye communyon sytting, and the Germans standing or going, and [he] mislyked the order of receaving the same here knelinge," he was severely censured for speaking against the statutes of the realm. Another minister was charged with receiving the sacrament "unreverentlye, standing upon his feet," and still another was threatened with deprivation of his office because, it was charged, "he receyveth the Communyon neyther syttinge nor standinge but bowing his kne towardes the grownde at the receyving thereof." The Puritans insisted on receiving communion in their pews, where it could not readily be observed whether they sat or knelt.

When the bishops of the Church of England, supported by the crown, refused to make concessions on this and other points, large numbers of dissenters left the state church to become Presbyterians, Congregationalists, and Baptists. Until the beginning of the nineteenth century it was customary for Presbyterian communicants to proceed to the front of the church and sit down at a table spread there. Since that time not only Presbyterians but also Congregationalists, Baptists, and others in Britain and America have remained seated in their pews, and the elements have been distributed to them there by elders or deacons, the minister presiding behind the communion table.

In the ancient church it had been the practice for communicants to take the cup and bread into their own hands when these were offered to them. When in the course of the Middle Ages attention was increasingly riveted on the elements, priests put the chalice to the lips of communicants and inserted the bread directly into their mouths, not only to eliminate "desecration" by dropping or spilling but also to prevent people from taking the sacred host home and using it to practice witchcraft and black magic. Although in theory the Reformation repudiated the notions which lay behind the introduction of a method of distribution in which "communicants are treated like helpless patients to whom one administers medicine," to employ the words of Professor August Kaehler, in practice Lutherans and Anglicans adhered conservatively to the medieval way of handling the chalice. However, many of them returned to the more ancient custom of receiving the bread in their hands. Instead of such individual administration of the elements by a minister, Presbyterians and others passed a plate of cubed bread and a common cup from hand to hand among the communicants. This seemed to them to be more in keeping with the words, "Take this, and divide it among yourselves" (Luke 22:17).

The common cup soon became a problem among Protestants—not among Roman Catholics, for wine was not given to Catholic laymen after the close of the

Middle Ages, as we have seen. First an esthetic objection to the use of a common chalice made itself felt. Sensitive people were offended when dirty or diseased persons drank from the same cup from which they were about to drink. A farmer's wife declared, "I no longer go to large communions where there are many men. All of our men chew tobacco, and since the women commune after them, the latter receive an evil-smelling mixture of wine and tobacco to drink." Such an esthetic objection was then followed by a hygienic one. What had before been vague intimations about the way in which diseases may be communicated received support from newer knowledge of germs. Physicians and health officers campaigned against the use of common drinking vessels in public places, in schools, and in homes. In time fountains and individual paper cups replaced common tin cups wherever water was dispensed, and rigid regulations were introduced for the effective cleansing of glasses and cups in which other beverages were publicly served. Even members of a family ceased to use the same drinking vessel.

It was inevitable that such esthetic and hygienic considerations should be applied to the continued use of a common cup in the administration of the Lord's Supper. As a matter of fact, some precautions had long been observed. It had been customary since the sixteenth century to have one or more additional chalices and to use these for administration to persons who had discernible facial diseases. It had also become common by the eighteenth century to turn and wipe the chalice so that no two communicants would put their lips to the same part of the rim. It was later pointed out, however, that wiping with a linen napkin was not an effective way of dealing with germs and that turning the chalice helped little since infection could be carried by the wine which the lips had touched as well as by the edge of the chalice. When it was argued that one should trust God and continue to use a common cup, the reply was given that not to observe intelligent precautions would be to tempt God. When it was argued that the common cup has important symbolical meaning, it was pointed out that the symbol of the common loaf ("we all partake of the same loaf," 1 Cor. 10:17) had long since been abandoned by the use either of wafers or of cubes of bread. A common cup, it was said, had been customary for ordinary drinking purposes in the first century but was no longer customary.

Such were the arguments pro and con. Anglicans refused to alter the inherited form of administration. Many Lutherans were similarly conservative, but other Lutherans, especially in North America, have adopted individual cups since the last decades of the nineteenth century. The same has been true, in Europe as well as in America, of most Presbyterians, Methodists, Congregationalists, Baptists, and others. The substitution of individual for common cups is only one of many changes which have been introduced in the administration and reception of the Lord's Supper, as we have noticed. As a matter of fact, it is a recent change and one that has probably not as yet run its full course.

FREQUENCY OF COMMUNION

The New Testament records no command of Christ or of the apostles to indicate how often one should participate in the Lord's Supper. However, there are some indications concerning the practice of primitive Christians. There appears to have been a weekly observance in some places (Acts 20:7), a daily observance in others (Acts 2:46). It is important to note that from the beginning there was no uniformity as to frequency. It is also important to remember, as we have had occasion to remark before, that in early times the Lord's Supper had social and charitable aspects which later fell away, and therefore one must be very cautious about equating the early Supper with that of later ages.

In the fourth century, when persecutions ceased and Christianity was given legal recognition in the Roman Empire, churches experienced a vast influx of converts. Intimate gatherings of Christians were transformed into large public assemblies. The fact that greater numbers of people were thronging into churches inevitably affected the atmosphere of public worship, and it was no longer possible to observe the Lord's Supper in all respects as it had been done before. Often the sacrament continued to be observed every Sunday, but it was no longer customary, as it had been before, for everybody to commune. This was both the cause and the effect of a growing tendency to transform the Lord's Supper into a cultic act of sacrifice, performed by priests in behalf of the people, to secure special favors from God. Access to the sacrament was made more difficult when fasting before communion was recommended and then required. Moreover, worthiness of reception was so defined under the influence of an ideal of celibacy as to exclude men and boys who had had nocturnal emissions during the previous night, women who were menstruating, and husbands and wives who had engaged in sexual intercourse. To arrest the resulting tendency on the part of the people to avoid reception of the sacrament altogether, the Council of Agde required in the year 506 that lay people should commune at least three times a year, at Christmas, Easter, and Pentecost. By the year 1215 frequency of reception had declined so much that the Fourth Lateran Council lowered the minimum expectation to one communion a year, at Easter.

This decline in frequency of communion was accompanied by a vast increase in the frequency of priestly celebration. Since a sacrifice was said to be made to God by a priest in behalf of the people, it was not regarded as essential for the people to participate or even to be present. People paid to have priests say masses for them in order to secure special favors from God—protection from pestilence, insurance of success in business, shortening of a stay in purgatory, etc. Because the people had many needs and desires there was a great increase in such votive masses at the same time that there was a sharp decline in frequency of communion.

The Reformation reversed this. Votive masses were prohibited among Protestants on the ground that they were in conflict with the nature and purpose of the sacrament. Instead of a multitude of masses without communicants, therefore, comparatively few celebrations of the Lord's Supper were held in which, as the Augsburg Confession expressed it, "the people are accustomed to receive the sacrament together." Instead of having a priest "celebrate," a large company of people "celebrated." Instead of some fifty masses a week in an average parish church at the close of the Middle Ages, the Lord's Supper was now generally observed among Lutherans and Anglicans only once a week at most. Among the German, Dutch, and French Reformed and among Presbyterians it was observed only once a month or four times a year. This drastic reduction in the frequency of administration was accompanied by an increase in reception. Instead of communing only once a year, as had been customary, Protestants received the sacrament an average of about four times a year. This was in accord with an opinion which Luther expressed in the preface to his *Small Catechism*: "Anyone who does not desire to receive the sacrament at least three or four times a year despises the sacrament and is no Christian." It was also in accord with a statute in Cambridge, England, which required that the Lord's Supper be administered on the first or second Sunday in every month and that all "shall communicate four times in the year at least."

In the course of the sixteenth century, and then also in succeeding centuries, administration was accommodated to reception and not vice versa. That is to say, the Lord's Supper was made available as often as would be necessary to make it possible for people to receive the Sacrament conveniently at their accustomed frequency.

In large urban parishes with many communicants there were often more opportunities for reception than in small country parishes with few communicants. In the eighteenth century frequency of communion declined, partly as a result of the removal of earlier civil penalties for abstention from the sacrament and partly as a result of the general religious apathy which marked the age of reason. Many ceased to attend church altogether, and those who continued to attend received the sacrament only once or twice a year. Under these circumstances it no longer seemed necessary to have communion services as often as before; the Lord's Supper was celebrated four, six, or eight times a year in most Protestant churches.

Since the beginning of the nineteenth century revived interest in the sacrament has taken a variety of forms. Many Roman Catholics still observe the custom of communing only once a year, but more frequent communion has been encouraged, and some devout Catholics commune monthly. Under the influence of the Oxford Movement, which represented a romantic return to ancient and medieval practices among Anglicans, the Lord's Supper began to be celebrated in many parishes not only every Sunday but also on weekdays. Relatively few communicants participated, however, and this prevented the corporate character of the sacrament from coming to expression and also exposed Anglicans to the charge of multiplying priestly celebration for its own sake. Revival of the sacrament took a different turn among Disciples of Christ, a new church body which was born on the American frontier in the first half of the nineteenth century. Regarding practices mentioned in the New Testament as normative, and believing that weekly communion was uniformly observed in the apostolic church, the Disciples and some others have received the sacrament every Sunday.

Even if it could be established that there had been a uniform practice in the apostolic age, Lutherans have in principle been as little interested in making such a pattern of frequency normative as they have been interested in reproducing other details of primitive practice. However, among Lutherans as among Presbyterians, Reformed, Methodists, and others there has been a modest overall increase in frequency of communion since the nineteenth century. Where previously observed, quarterly celebrations of the sacrament have often been supplanted by bi-monthly or monthly celebrations, and reception has increased again to an average of about four times a year.

In our time the question of frequency of communion has for some people become a matter of central importance. The more often one communes, it has been claimed, the more pious one will be. There is no evidence to support such a correlation between quantity in terms of reception and quality in terms of Christian life. To suppose that there is may well betray a view of the sacrament which makes of it the swallowing of some sort of impersonal "medicine of immortality."

There are others who propose that we are under obligation today to receive the sacrament as often as Christians received it in the past. However, as we have seen, frequency of communion has varied from age to age and from people to people, and it has varied partly for practical reasons and partly because of changing understandings of what the Lord's Supper is. More frequent communion is to be expected in churches (like the Roman Catholic, Eastern Orthodox, and Anglican) which hold that it is in the sacrament alone that Christ is present and active, and somewhat less frequent communion is to be expected in churches (like the Lutheran, Reformed, Presbyterian, and Methodist) which hold that Christ is salvatorily present and active in the preaching of the Gospel as well as in the sacrament.

An appeal to history will not provide us with an easy answer to the question of frequency, but it should help us to understand the experience of the church and to guard us against a slavish imitation of any part of the past without regard to the conditions and circumstances which obtained at that time.

REFLECTIONS IN RETROSPECT

Many things that might have been profitably touched upon have had to be omitted in this brief review of past and present practices connected with the Lord's Supper. Moreover, it has been possible to mention only the most important factors which have contributed to the adoption of one or another usage. Enough has been said, however, to show that the outward observance of the Lord's Supper has been subject to constant change. It should also have become clear that as a consequence the sacrament is nowhere observed today exactly as it was in the primitive church.

When some radicals on the left wing of the Reformation insisted that details of the primitive practice must be restored, Luther pointedly asked if this would not require that the Lord's Supper be held only in Jerusalem, only in an upper room, only in the evening, and only with participants reclining. None of the major churches of Christendom ever attempted quite so radical a reproduction of the externals of the Last Supper because it had to be acknowledged that changes in outward observance had occurred even within the apostolic age. However, some were reluctant to allow the propriety of such changes after New Testament times.

More characteristic of Christendom as a whole has been the contention that change and development are not only permissible but inevitable. The Roman Catholic

Council of Trent expressed it this way in 1562: "In the dispensation of the sacraments . . . the church may ordain or change whatever things it may deem most expedient for the profit of those who receive, or for the veneration of the sacraments, according to the difference of circumstances, times, and places." Much the same thing was asserted, to take a second example, in the Lutheran Formula of Concord in 1577: "The church of God in every place and in every time has the right, authority, and power to change, to reduce, or to increase ceremonies according to circumstances, . . . as at any time may seem to be most profitable, beneficial, and salutary for good order, Christian discipline, evangelical decorum, and the edification of the church." Although both of these statements make allowances for development and change, the contexts in which the statements were made need to be noticed.

The first question that must be asked is, Who may make such changes? Both statements refer to the church, but the church is not thought of in the same way. For Roman Catholics the church tends to be conceived of in clerical terms, and it is ultimately the pope who has authority to make changes. A recent instance is a papal directive on the times of day Mass may or may not be said. For Protestants, on the other hand, the church is the community of believers, laymen as well as clergymen, and a local congregation is as much and as fully the church as the larger ecclesiastical body of which it is a part. Authority to make changes in external practice rests on the consent of such Christian communities.

The second question that must be asked is, How binding are such changes? For Roman Catholics the pope or commissions responsible to him issue directives demanding conformity. Even when deviations in practice are permitted, exceptions are specifically prescribed. Uniformity tends to be an end in itself, as the requirement that Latin be used in the Mass suggests, and this uniformity is achieved by obedience to authority. For Protestants, on the other hand, man's relationship to God in faith frees him from the necessity of such submissive conformity. "It is not necessary," the Augsburg Confession asserts, "that human traditions or rites and ceremonies, instituted by men, should be alike everywhere." However, the love which comes with or from faith ministers to the needs of fellow men and seeks agreement for the sake of good order. This is achieved not by compulsion but by consent, not by furtive machinations but by open discussion.

The third question that must be asked is, What are the grounds on which changes are made? The Catholic tendency is to be guided by precedent. The appeal is to the evolving tradition of the past. When traditions are found to be contradictory (we have noted many cases of conflicting precedents) appeal is made to the "living tradition" said to be embodied in the papacy. The trouble with this, said the radicals of the sixteenth century, is that most of the developments since the apostolic age represent departure from true Christianity; the church can return to the right path only by limiting itself to what is expressly prescribed in the New Testament. The major Protestant position differed from both of these. It has been neither traditionalistic nor biblicistic while having due regard both for tradition and for the Bible. The ultimate criterion for practice is the

Word of God, and this is the message of God's judgment and grace to which the Bible bears witness. No practice may contradict the Word of God; every practice must express or exhibit the Word of God, the proclamation of which is the church's mission, and man's response to it. This has direct bearing on practices connected with the Lord's Supper because, as Luther put it, this sacrament is "a brief summary of the Gospel."

What this means is that every way of doing things— every symbol, action, gesture, or ceremony—is in itself neutral. It is an *adiaphoron,* a matter of indifference. But the context in which it is used and the meaning which it therefore conveys can make it helpful or misleading, and in this sense right or wrong. The picture of a saint, Luther once suggested, may in itself be good, but if it is used to pray to the saint it is not good. So, to take an example which we have encountered above, there is nothing wrong in itself with the tinkling of a bell; but if a sanctus bell or sacring bell is rung at the moment of "consecration," it declares or implies something that no Protestant can believe. Unless symbols and actions are to be stripped of all meaning (and this would be tragic), they must be allowed to retain the significance they have acquired by use and association.

Frequent change and sudden innovation in practice are undesirable because they militate against good order and highlight what is secondary at the expense of what is central in the sacrament. Conservative adherence to tradition can also be disastrous, for not every practice of the past is edifying today. The same action, when simply transplanted to a different age and culture, can suggest a meaning quite at variance with the original intention. Other practices of the past would not be suitable today for a different reason: they grew up in times when there was a very different understanding of the Lord's Supper, and they reflect and set forth this different understanding. Actions communicate as well as words. The question that must always be asked is, What do they communicate?

The history of the church shows that it is possible to become so preoccupied with outward forms that the real significance of the Lord's Supper as proclamation of the Gospel is lost sight of. The church both in the East and in the West was adopting all sorts of meticulous regulations to specify how sacramental bread and wine should be made at the very time when the sacrament was being transformed into a sacrifice. The shell was preserved but the kernel was lost. Our concern must be the reverse of this: we must be willing to adapt and change the shell so that the kernel may be preserved in a setting suited to it in the time, place, and circumstances in which we find ourselves.

The kernel must never be isolated from the whole proclamation of the church. This is what Luther meant when he declared that the Lord's Supper is a brief summary of the Gospel. Like all oral witness to Christ, every observance of the Lord's Supper is a testimony to Christ, who gave himself for us and for our salvation. Just as the oral witness not only declares something but also effects what it declares, so the action in the Sacrament not only symbolizes something but also effects what it symbolizes. In intimate table fellowship Christ unites himself with the believer, and in Christ the believer is united with his fellow believer. Christ is at once the Giver and the Gift. Therefore, as Luther put it in his *Small Catechism,* "the forgiveness of sins, life, and salvation are given to us in the sacrament."

Type used in this book
Body, 10 on 13 Caledonia
Display, Times Roman
Paper: Spring Grove Antique "R"